Basics of Energy Efficient Living

Living

A Beginner's Guide to Alternative Energy and Home Energy Savings

By
Lonnie Wibberding

Big Fish Publishing Inc
Telford, PA 18969

Published By
Big Fish Publishing Inc
51 West Summit Avenue
Telford, PA 18969
www.BigFishBooks.com

Cover Photography
istockphoto

Printed in the United States of America
ISBN 0-9777982-3-2

Dedication

I would like to dedicate this book to
Jeff Staddon. He has encouraged me to write
many times and for that I'm thankful.

Table of Contents

Introduction

Energy is interesting. I noticed this for the first time living in Central Alaska. As winter came my electric bill shot past $200 a month. Not to be outdone the cost of fuel oil past $300 a month. $500 a month just for energy! I decided there had to be a better way.

I'm happy to say there is. I never solved my energy problems in Central Alaska, but in the years that followed my interest in energy never left. If I lived there again I could do better – much better.

My first goal in writing this book is to teach you how to design an energy efficient house. Whether you want to improve the house you have or build your own, you will find helpful, step-by-step information. This is what the first part of this book is about.

Hopefully you will want to go all the way and find your energy in other places than retail. If you want to know your options part two is for you. Here we look at how much energy is in each resource and what it takes to get it.

The third section, *The* System, we put all the pieces together. We look at storage systems, how to store the energy you find.

I hope you find this little book an invaluable reference guide for your own exploration into alternative energy sources. If when you are done reading it you know how to design your house to be energy efficient and how to get the energy you need to run it I've done my job.

Part I – Basic Principles

Chapter 1

What is Energy?

What is energy? It seems like a simple question -- almost too simple. Who cares? Let's get on to something practical. But wait a second. Before you skip this chapter there is some exciting stuff here. Two important concepts that will help you understand everything else. The first is:

> ### *Energy is the ability to do work!*

Now aren't you glad you stayed with me? You probably feel your life getting more exciting even now. If you are having a little trouble applying this new insight let me help you. What does it mean when we say, *"Energy is the ability to do work."*?

For example, you have a piano to move. It's been sitting in the basement for the last month waiting to be moved up to your living room. The problem is you don't want to move it by yourself. In fact you are not even sure it is possible for you to move it by yourself. It is too much *work*. It requires too much *energy*. More *energy* than you have.

As you sit at your piano contemplating heavy objects and two story houses you begin to think. There are two options: Either reduce the workload or increase the energy. You can divide up the work into smaller more manageable sizes. You still have your neighbor Bob's chain saw in the garage. But divorce is expensive. The other option seems better – increase the energy.

You have three friends, Bill, Bob, and Brad who have about the same amount of energy as you. If you pool your energy maybe you can move it. So you call them up and attempt to *harness* their energy to do some *work* by moving your piano. Your success to do so will depend on several factors such as whether Bob remembers you are the one who never returned his chainsaw. If he does remember, the *cost* of harnessing his energy may be higher than it's worth. (We'll talk more about the cost of harnessing energy in later chapters.)

So you call and get your three friends to come over. It's enough for the work that needs to be done. Success – piano in the living room!

Energy, whatever it is your trying to do, is the ability to do work. More work, more energy is needed. Less work, less energy is needed.

This concept is important if you own a piano, but even non-piano owners can make use of it. There is energy all around us. The book on the high shelf can have a string tied around it. When it is pushed off the shelf the string can wind a clock. The book has energy waiting to be used. The wind howling past your house can be caught in a sheet to move a sailboat (work) or turn a wind turbine to produce electricity. The sun shining through your window can strike a solar panel to produce electricity and do work. Or it can be focused on a pipe with water in it to produce steam to push a piston to do work.

As we begin to think of the things around us as potential sources of energy suddenly a whole new world emerges. One begins to realize there is plenty of energy all around us to supply our needs if we are creative enough to use it.

If one option is too costly chances are there is another energy source close by. If Bob is still mad about the chainsaw there is always Jim across the street. With so many options we don't have to get stuck on just one.

In addition to the idea that *energy is the ability to do work* comes a second basic principle:

Energy can transfer forms

This is as important as the first principle and probably more exciting. This means it doesn't matter what form you encounter energy in as long as you have a way to get it to the form you need you can still use it.

There are four kinds (or forms) of energy we will discuss. Any one of them can be transferred into any of the other three.

Energy Forms

Mechanical energy is the energy it takes to move something. A waterfall produces mechanical energy from the force of the water falling. It is what moves the wheels in your car. It has to do with motion. It is measured in Horsepower (hp).

Electrical energy is, as the name implies, the energy contained in electricity. This is usually measured in watts or kilowatts. When measured over time it is measured in watt-hours or kilowatt-hours (kWh).

Thermal Energy is the energy found in heat. It is measured in British Thermal Units (btu).

Light Energy is the energy found in light. It can be measured several ways. For us it is easiest to use the unit btus per square foot.

The principle that energy can transfer forms is the basis for an energy system. The job of the system is to take the energy in one form and transfer it to the form we want. For instance, if we want electricity and we have heat our system will be designed to take heat energy and turn it into electrical energy.

We can do this several ways. If the heat (thermal energy) is at a high enough temperature it can be used to create steam, which could turn a turbine (mechanical), which connected to a generator could produce electricity (electrical). This is not a direct transfer from thermal to electrical but it does the job.

Another way we could make the transfer is through what is called a thermal couple. This is made of two dissimilar metals which when heated create an electrical current. However, thermal couples are very inefficient. In other words, the energy you get out in electricity is a small percentage of what you put in, in heat.

Efficiency of Transferring Forms

Each time we transfer from one form to another we usually lose some energy. Not all the energy goes where we want it. On the low end a solar panel generally captures only 12-14% of the energy available from the sun. Changing light energy to electrical energy is not very efficient through a solar cell. Does that mean you shouldn't do it? It depends on your situation. It may be worth it to you after considering the other options.

Among the higher efficient conversions is electricity to heat. Generally it's about 95% efficient. However, just because it's an efficient transfer doesn't mean it's most cost effective. For example, with the cost of electricity, using an electric hot water heater may not be a good choice. Even though most of your energy goes into heating the hot water, the cost of that electricity could be prohibitive.

To understand this a little better we need to introduce our third and final principle for this chapter:

Energy is measurable

Measuring Energy

Whether we look at the mechanical energy from a waterfall, or the heat from the sun, or the spinning of a turbine in the wind, or climbing your stairs; we can measure it. Not only can we measure energy, we can change units of measurement to find how much heat we can get for a certain electrical input, or how much electricity can be produced from a waterfall. We could also figure out how much heat we can get from the sun, or how much heat my stove will put out for each piece of wood I put in.

Energy Units

There are three units of measurement we will use in this book which will help us understand energy. They are: btu, kilowatt (kW), and horsepower (hp).

BTU

A btu or British Thermal Unit is the heat required to raise one pound of water 1 degree Fahrenheit.

If I have a pound of water that is 34°F and I raise it to 35°F, I add one btu to it. If I have a pound of water at 85°F and raise it to 86°F, I add one btu to it. Any temperature my pound of water is at, if I add one btu to it the temperature will go up one degree Fahrenheit. It works the other way too. If I have a pound of water at 85°F and let it cool to 84°F I lose one btu.

A pound of water is just over a pint (two cups). One gallon of water weighs 8.333 lbs.

The Cost of a Shower

To understand how energy is measured let's look at a real life example. How much energy is used to take a shower and how much does it cost?

To find how much energy is used we need to know two things: How much the water is heated and how many gallons you will use?

Do Try This At Home!

You will need:
✓ Thermometer
✓ 4 cup measuring cup
✓ Watch with second hand
✓ Oil, gas, or electric bill (depending on what kind of hot water you have).

The water comes into your house cold. Whatever the ground temperature is will be about what your water temperature is. The hot water heater heats this water to about 120°F. Not all the water coming out of the showerhead is from the hot water heater. It is mixed with cold water to create the temperature we want. Part of each gallon is hot water and part is cold. We could calculate how much is each but we really don't have to. What we need to know is how many btus (how much heat) was added to each gallon coming out of the showerhead to bring it up to the temperature we want. Figuring this out is easier than it seems.

Remember we said a btu is the energy it takes to heat one pound of water 1°F. By figuring out how much each gallon of water coming out of the showerhead is heated we will know how much energy is used.

Here's how you do it. Grab your 4-cup measuring cup and thermometer. Go to your bathroom and adjust the shower to the temperature and pressure you like. Now catch the shower stream with the measuring cup and record its temperature. Empty the cup and fill it up again, timing how long it takes to fill. Then turn the shower all the way cold and record the temperature of the cold water coming in.

Notes

Preferred shower temp. (in °F) _____

Cold water temp. (in °F) _____

Seconds to fill a 4 cup container _____

Length of shower in minutes _____

Subtracting the cold water temperature from the shower temperature will give us the difference. My shower temperature is 110°F and my cold water is 50°F. The difference is 60°F (110-50=60). For every pound of water I use in my shower it will take 60 btus to heat it to the temperature I like.

For convenience, we will convert pounds of water to gallons. There are 8.333 pounds of water in a gallon. So for each gallon of water I use, it will take (8.333 x 60) 500 btus.

The next step is to find how many gallons of water are used during a shower. We will use the seconds it took to fill your cup to figure this out.

For example, when I did this it took 6 ¼ seconds to fill my 4-cup container. We multiply this by 4 to get gallons. (16 cups to a gallon). This gives us 25 seconds to fill a gallon. Since there are 60 seconds in a minute, 60 divided by 25 gives us the flow rate in gallons per minute (g.p.m.). In my case it's 2.4 g.p.m.

I can multiply my flow rate by the 500 btus/gallon we find earlier and find the btus per minute used. In my case I use 1,200 btus for each minute a take a shower.

To find how much energy a whole shower uses I multiply the minute energy consumption by the length of shower. In my case a 10 minute shower uses 12,000 btus.

Review	
Shower temp – cold water temp	= Difference temp
Difference temp x 8.333	= btus per gallon
60 / (Seconds to fill 4-cups x 4)	= Gallons per minute
btus per gallon x gallons per minute	= btus per minute
btus per minute x shower length	= btus per shower

Kilowatt

Before we finish calculating the cost of a shower we need to introduce a second unit of measure. It's the Kilowatt or Kilowatt-hour (kWh).

One kilowatt is 1,000 watts. Watts and kilowatts are usually used when we talk about electricity. A Kilowatt-hour is the amount of energy one kilowatt gives over an hour. Ten 100 watt light bulbs would require 1,000 watts (10 x 100) or 1 kilowatt. If we turned these on for one hour they would consume one kilowatt-hour of energy. There are 3,414.4 btus for each Kilowatt-hour.

Let's go back to the shower. For those of us with an electric hot water heater we need to figure out how many kilowatt-hours we use. If my shower took 12,000 btus and I used electricity to heat the water, how much did the shower cost?

1. Each btu is equal to 0.000292875 kWh (Kilowatt hours. The energy 1,000 watts delivers in 1 hour).
2. Multiply by 12,000 btus gives us 3.51 kWh.
3. We must divide this by an efficiency factor of 95% (0.95) This is the efficiency of converting electricity to heat. This gives us 3.70 kWh
4. I pay $0.11 per kWh to my electric company. Such a shower would cost me $0.41 ($0.11 x 3.70).

It doesn't seem like much but over a month that's $12.21. Four people in your family could cost you $49 just for showers!

If you have a gas or oil water heater you can find how much it costs by knowing how much you pay per btu. Natural gas will be billed in cubic feet and oil by the gallon.

There are 142,600 btu/gallon in heating oil but most oil furnaces are only about 80% efficient. Count on getting about 114,000 usable btus per gallon of oil.

Natural gas heaters are usually more efficient. You can depend on getting about 1,000 btus per cubic foot of natural gas.

Whatever your energy source, figure out how much you are paying per btu, then how many btus you use which will give you the cost of a shower. Fun stuff!

Horsepower

The third energy unit is horsepower (hp). It is used to measure mechanical energy. Horsepower was developed when James Watt needed a standard to measure how much work a horse could do in a period of time. With some refinement one horsepower become 33,000 foot-lbs per minute. As a horse pulled a load out of a mineshaft through a series of pulleys, it was discovered he could lift about 33,000 lbs one foot in one minute. As the pulleys were geared differently the same energy could be used in another way 1,000 lbs could be pulled 33 feet (33 feet x 1,000 lbs = 33,000 foot-lbs) Or 33 lbs could be pulled 1,000 feet. Any combination could be used within reason. (Getting a horse to pull 1 lb 33,000 feet in one minute could be impractical). With this standard a unit of measurement was developed to measure any mechanical energy.

To help understand this a little better, imagine you have built a platform in a tree 100 feet off the ground. You have rigged a pulley system attached to a generator to let you down from the tree. The idea is to transform the energy of the weight of your body falling into something useful. You want to know how much energy you will generate.

Before I ask you why you built a platform so far up let's do some calculations. Since I don't know how much you weigh I'll guess 150 lbs. You are going to fall 100 feet (slowly I hope). First we figure out how many foot-lbs you generate. A fairly simple calculation. 150 lbs (you) multiplied by the distance you fall (100 feet) equals 15,000 foot-lbs.

How much power is that?
At this rate you would generate 339 watts of power for one minute.

One horsepower = 746 watts
0.455 hp x 746 = 339 watts

Not a great amount of energy but energy nonetheless. Enough to illuminate a few light bulbs so you can see where you are falling . . .

We know one horsepower is 33,000 foot-lbs per minute. So if it takes you one minute to fall you will generate 0.455hp (15,000/33,000 foot-lbs).

Summary

Energy is the ability to do work. Whether it's lighting a bulb or moving a piano, if there is work to be done energy is what will do it. Energy can change forms although usually we lose some when we do. And energy is measurable. We can calculate how much we will need for each application.

Reference

Btus in common fuels

Natural Gas	1,000 btu/ft^3
Propane	337,479 btu/gallon
Heating Oil #2	142,600 btu/gallon
Heating Oil #1	139,100 btu/gallon

Conversions

One btu =
- ✓ 0.000292875 Kilowatt hours.
- ✓ 0.000393 Horsepower hours

One kilowatt-hour =
- ✓ 3414.4 btus
- ✓ 1.341 Horsepower-hours

One horsepower-hour =
- ✓ 2546.1 btus
- ✓ 0.7457 Kilowatt-hours.

Chapter 2

Energy Conservation

When you plan an energy system for your home the first step is conservation. The easiest way to bring the amount of energy needed closer to the energy available is to reduce the amount of energy needed. Conserve energy. The less you use, the less infrastructure you will need to support your lifestyle. Conserving doesn't always mean doing with less.

There are three ways to conserve. First is to reduce how much is consumed – this does mean living with less. Instead of taking a 15-minute shower take 5 minutes. Turn lights off when leaving a room and turn the thermostat down a few degrees. The second is to reduce the amount of energy leaving the house. This includes more insulation or sealing air leaks. The third is to *recover* the energy leaving the house. This is essentially the same as the second but requires thinking along different lines.

Just like your financial budget, trimming your energy budget is easier in some areas than others. Most of us use energy in three main area: heating (or cooling), hot water, and electricity.

Heating

When we think of heating many times we think about the temperature inside but not outside. But the key to planning a heating (or cooling) system is to find the difference in temperature between inside and out. This temperature spread is what will try to cool or heat your house when you don't want it to. If your house is 70°F inside and it's also 70°F outside you don't have to worry about keeping the heat in. No insulation – no problem. However, if you want the temperature inside to be 70°F and the temperature outside is 50°F we have a problem. The problem is 20°F. (The difference between 50°F and 70°F)

Our job then is to design a house, which keeps as much cold as possible out and as much heat as possible in. (Here we discuss keeping heat in. However, the principles are the same to keep it out.)

Building a House

To understand the energy concepts in this book we will begin now to build a house. There is a worksheet in a few pages where you will be able to plan for your own house, but as an example we will design one as we go.

The main concern in our design is conservation of energy. How can we keep the most energy in the house while still maintaining a good living environment? Of course if we are not concerned about the environment of the house we could completely seal off all airflow and save a lot of energy. But humans have this habit of breathing which would soon fill the house with carbon dioxide and take all the oxygen. Plants love carbon dioxide and give off oxygen in its place. But to find the perfect balance between plant life and humans is beyond the scope of this book. We will assume we want air exchange.

As we think of this idea of an energy efficient house we begin with the structure. Every surface that is between the outside and inside is a place where energy can be transferred (lost). If we can minimize the surface area that meets the outside we can minimize heat lost.

How do we get the least surface touching the outside air with the most room inside? What shape will be most efficient? A quick example will illustrate. (The symbol ft^2 means square feet and the symbol ft^3 means cubic feet.)

If we build a house 10 feet tall, 2 feet wide and 50 feet long we get the following:
- ❖ Inside cubic feet (10 x 2 x 50) is 1000 ft^3
- ❖ Outside wall surface is 1,240 ft^2
    - ○ Floor and ceiling each (2 x 50) 100 ft^2
    - ○ Walls
        - ▪ 2 @ (10 x 50) 500 ft^2
        - ▪ 2 @ (2 x 10) 20 ft^2

This gives us an inside cubic foot to outside square foot ratio of 1.2. 1.2 square feet of outside wall for every 1 cubic foot of inside space.

If we build a house 10 feet tall, 10 feet wide and 10 feet long we get the same cubic feet inside:
- ❖ Inside cubic feet (10 x 10 x 10) is 1000 ft^3
- ❖ Outside wall surface is 600 ft^2
    - ○ Floor and ceiling each (10 x 10) 100 ft^2
    - ○ Walls
        - ▪ 4 @ (10 x 10) 100 ft^2

This is a 0.6 ratio. We only have 600 ft^2 of outside wall – less than half as much to insulate. A cube is the most efficient shape. The closer you can get all the walls to match in size, the more inside room you will have for each outside square foot of wall.

So for our sample house let's build a two-story house. We will use a small floor plan to conserve space. This will give us less room we have to heat and will give us a cube shaped house (or close to it to reduce wall area). If we build it 24 ft x 24 ft we will have 576 ft^2 on the first floor and the same on the second. 1,152 ft^2 is not a huge house but adequate for many people. Allowing for a standard 8 ft ceiling and a foot for the floor joists on the second floor the height of each outside wall is 17 ft.

Starting on page 37 there is a worksheet for each wall in your house. You will be able to fill in the information as we go along.

R-Value & Conduction

We've thought about the shape of our house and decided on the best structure for our needs. For our sample house we have 2,784 ft² of outside surface to figure out how to stop heat from escaping through.

There are many building materials to build a house from. If you like a lot of windows we could make the whole structure out of glass. However, glass may not be the best choice when we think of energy efficiency. Each material conducts heat or lets heat pass through it at a different rate. This is called conduction. Some materials, like copper, have high heat conductivity. If we build a house out of copper we would have a good idea what the outside temperature is since it would be very close to what it was inside. On the other hand, some materials conduct heat very poorly. Fiberglass insulation for instance lets heat pass through very slow.

In order to compare a range of materials and calculate heat loss, r-value and u-value were developed. You may have heard of r-value. We talk about it when we think of insulating a house. Fiberglass insulation comes with an r-value rating (r-11, r-19, r-30, etc). What does it mean?

Let's start with u-value. U-value is the number of btus which will pass through one square foot of material (wall, ceiling, etc) in one hour for each degree difference in temperature of the two sides. If the difference is 1°F and two btus pass through one square foot in an hour, the u-value is 2. If ten btus pass through the u-value is 10.

R-value is one over u-value or the reciprocal of u-value. If the insulation in the wall is r-13 this means that 1/13th of a btu will go through the insulation per hour for every degree Fahrenheit the temperature is different on the two sides.

So if you have a window 4ft x 3ft with an r-value of 2, it means it has a u-value of 1/2 (1 over r-value) and will lose 1/2 a btu per hour per ft^2 for every degree Fahrenheit difference.

R-Values for various building materials & Components:

Material	Thickness	R-Value
2x4 stud	3 ½"	4
2x6 stud	5 ½"	6.5
2x10 joist	9 ½"	10.8
2x12 joist	11 ½"	13
Drywall	½"	0.45
Drywall	5/8"	0.56
Fiberglass Bat.	3 ½"	11
Fiberglass Bat.	6"	19
Plywood	½"	0.62
Plywood	¾"	0.93
Polyurethane	1"	6.25
Windows		2 – 4

Standard Complete Walls		
2x4 wall 16" centers[1]		10.43
2x4 wall 24" centers		10.92
2x6 wall 16" centers		17.10
2x6 wall 24" centers		18.24

Here's a question. If the temperature outside is 40°F and inside 70°F, how many btus are lost per hour through the glass of the window?

1. The r-value is 2 so for each square foot we lose 1/2 a btu per hour per degree Fahrenheit.
2. The window is 12 ft^2 (4ft x 3ft). Since we lose ½ a btu for each square foot we lose 6 btus per hour per °F difference (1/2 btu x 12ft^2).
3. The difference is 30°F (70°F - 40°F).
4. 6 btus x 30°F is <u>180 btus per hour</u>.

You can do the same calculation for your walls. However, walls are hard to calculate because they have more components. The insulation has a certain r-value. The studs have another. The siding and drywall add more. (The r-value table on the previous page has calculated standard walls for you.)

Whatever way you can increase the r-value will save energy. Adding a thicker layer of insulation helps. So does using a material with a higher r-value per inch.

Walls

One of the problems we encounter when building is using wood studs. They are great for holding up a house and we need something to do that. Unfortunately the studs in a wall are not very efficient. A 2"x4" stud has an r-value of 4. If they are spaced every 16 inches (16 inch centers) the r-value of a square foot of wall with r-11 insulation is really only 9.4. (The 1 ½" of stud is r-4 and the 14 ½" of fiberglass insulation is r-11.)

There are several ways to reduce loses from this standard wall. One of the ways is to use 2"x6"studs. These give an r-value of 6, but more importantly give room for r-19 fiberglass insulation. This brings the average wall r-value up to r-15.8. This is 68% better than the 2"x4" walls. But what if you want even higher r-value in the walls?

One way to insulate even the studs is to use a polyurethane foam board on the outside of the house. This is installed under the siding. For each inch thickness of polyurethane an r-value of 6 ¼ is added. Just two inches would add r-12.5 to our r-15.8 for a total of 28.3. This is a 79% increase over the standard 2"x6" construction and a 301% increase over 2"x4" construction.

Another way to increase the r-value of our walls is to make a double wall and fill the inside with insulation. This way the studs don't go all the way through to the outside which stops them from transferring heat. This type of construction would allow for whatever space you want. The wall thickness is increased to accommodate the room for extra insulating material.

Studs never touch each other

There are other options as well. Straw bail construction is one. It boasts an r-value of 40!

Floors & Ceilings

Floors pose some of the same problems as walls. The floor joists conduct heat. But they are thicker than the walls and give more room for insulation. By using 2"x10"s for joists a floor could have r-30 fiberglass insulation for an average of r-25.7.

Ceilings are easier to insulate than walls or floors. Extra insulation can be laid above the rafter in the attic or blown in. The rafters are thicker, like floor joists, which makes the average possible r-value much higher. In years past ceilings were under insulated and to insulate your ceiling was the single most energy saving move you could make. Over the years however, ceilings became more insulated. Now in most cases the best energy saving move is to stop infiltration – which we will look at in a minute, but first windows.

Windows

Glass is not a good insulator. As we mentioned earlier, the r-value of a double paned window is about r-2. Some of the newer windows achieve an r-value as high as r-4. Compared to the rest of the building components of a house they are a major source of heat loss.

Realizing how much heat we were losing through the windows I suggested to my wife that we build a house without any windows. She suggested I could live in it by myself. I guess it goes back to the environment inside the house. You need light.

Windows are not all bad. South facing windows can actually add to the heat of the house as the sun shines in and strikes the surfaces of the room. But even south facing windows lose heat at night.

One way to reduce losses is to insulate your windows at night. If the window is insulated when there is no sun to shine in and when temperatures between inside and out are greatest, energy can be saved. There are many kinds of insulating shades that can be drawn at night. Some go on the inside, others outside. Some are ugly some are nice. The basic principle behind each is to slow down heat loss for the dark part of each 24-hour period. If you have r-4 windows, even a covering of r-4 would cut down your night losses through the windows in half. It's an easy way to save energy.

Putting it all together

Now that we've covered the basics, let's continue to build our sample house. We could start with any component. Since we were just talking about them let's start with the windows.

For convenience sake we will put two windows on each side of the house on each level. This will give us two windows upstairs on each side and two windows downstairs on each side for a total of sixteen windows. Each window will be 3ft x 3ft. Of course most houses wouldn't have all their windows uniform, but for ease of calculation we will this time. Let's go with the high quality windows with an r-value of 4.

Each window is 9 ft^2 for a total window area of 144 ft^2 for the whole house (9 ft^2 per window x 16 windows). Since we know the windows are r-4 we can calculate the heat loss through all the windows in the house (1/4th of a btu per square foot). For every degree °F difference in temperature we will lose **36 btus** per hour through the windows.

For the ceiling we will use blown-in insulation. We should be able to get an r-value over 40 easily. From our previous calculations you may remember we have 576 ft^2 of ceiling. Since we are using r-40 insulation we will multiply 576 ft^2 by 1/40 to get **14.4 btus.** For every degree difference in temperature from the inside and out we will lose 14.4 btus through the ceiling.

The floor is the same area as the ceiling. Using our previously calculated r-25 for the floor gives us **23 btus** through the floor (1/25 x 576).

If we use 2"x6" studs for the walls, r-19 insulation, and a 2" foam board on the outside, our walls should be about r-28. Each outside wall is 17ft x 24ft and we have four of them. This is 1632 ft^2 in total wall surface without windows. Subtracting for the windows (144 ft^2) gives us the real area of the walls at 1488 ft^2. Dividing this by the r-value of 28 gives us a loss of **53 btus** of energy through the walls each hour per °F difference between inside and outside temperature.

Sample house summary	
Windows	36 btus
Ceiling	15 btus
Floor	23 btus
Walls	53 btus
Total	127 btus/hr°F

If you put insulation over your windows of r-12 while you are not using them the 36 btu heat loss through them drops to 9 btus during that time, which is a savings of 21% overall. Of course this is impractical to have your windows boarded up all the time, but half the time (during the dark part) isn't so impractical. Just shutting those blinds at night could save 10% of the heat loss through conduction to the outside.

At 40°F outside and a desired temperature of 70°F inside, this house would require (without window blinds) **91,440 btus/day** to replace the energy that escapes through the house. (30°F difference in temperature times 127 btus/hr°F times 24 hours in a day).

Infiltration

Conduction through the material the house is not the only kind of heat loss. The second major factor in heating a home is infiltration – cold air creeping in.

You want some exchange of air for a healthy environment inside the house, but too much will cost you. As we will see later in this chapter, if we can control where the air enters and exits the house we can *recover* some of the heat that is leaving. So a tight house is helpful when we think of energy conservation. There is no magic formula to this. The main principle is to seal any place air can get in or out. This is generally done with a vapor barrier (6mm plastic sheet) installed right behind the drywall. Any holes which are put in the vapor barrier due to installation of outlets and other fixtures are sealed. This way most of the air exchange can be done through one central location.

Some claim 30% of the heat loss in a house is due to infiltration of cold air. To understand why this is and how important it is to you, we need to understand how much heat is in air

How much energy does it take to heat air? It depends on two factors: the air temperature and relative humidity. Relative humidity is the amount of water air can hold at a certain temperature. 100% humidity means the air is completely saturated or full of water. Warm air can hold more water than cool air. The following table shows how many btus it takes to heat one cubic foot of air at 0% to 100% humidity at a specific temperature

Specific heat for air

The units are btu/ft. This table assumes an elevation of sea level.

	0%	10%	20%	30%	40%	50%
10°F	0.02031	0.02032	0.02033	0.02033	0.02034	0.02035
20°F	0.01988	0.01990	0.01991	0.01992	0.01994	0.01995
30°F	0.01948	0.01950	0.01952	0.01954	0.01956	0.01958
40°F	0.01909	0.01912	0.01915	0.01918	0.01921	0.01924
50°F	0.01871	0.01875	0.01880	0.01885	0.01889	0.01894
60°F	0.01835	0.01841	0.01848	0.01854	0.01861	0.01867
70°F	0.01800	0.01809	0.01818	0.01827	0.01836	0.01845
80°F	0.01767	0.01779	0.01792	0.01804	0.01817	0.01829
90°F	0.01734	0.01752	0.01769	0.01786	0.01803	0.01820
100°F	0.01703	0.01727	0.01750	0.01773	0.01797	0.01820

	60%	70%	80%	90%	100%
10°F	0.02036	0.02037	0.02038	0.02039	0.02039
20°F	0.01997	0.01998	0.01999	0.02001	0.02002
30°F	0.01960	0.01963	0.01965	0.01967	0.01969
40°F	0.01927	0.01931	0.01934	0.01937	0.01940
50°F	0.01898	0.01903	0.01907	0.01912	0.01916
60°F	0.01874	0.01880	0.01886	0.01893	0.01899
70°F	0.01854	0.01863	0.01872	0.01881	0.01890
80°F	0.01842	0.01854	0.01866	0.01879	0.01891
90°F	0.01837	0.01854	0.01871	0.01888	0.01905
100°F	0.01843	0.01866	0.01890	0.01913	0.01936

Let's take our sample house and see how many btus we lose in one hour if the air in the house changes every hour.

1. Our sample house is 24ft x 24ft and 17ft in height if we include two stories with ceilings at 8ft plus a one foot space between floors. This gives us 9,792 ft^3.
2. We will assume the temperature outside is 40°F with a relative humidity of 70%. We find on the chart that 40°F air at 70% humidity requires 0.01931 btus for every cubic foot to heat. This is the requirement to raise it one degree.
3. We have a standard inside temperature of 70°F so we are raising each cubic foot of air 30°F. 0.01931 btus x 30°F is 0.5793 btus/ft^3.
4. There are 9,792 cubic feet of air space in the house so this will require 5,673 btus for every air exchange (9,792 x 0.5793 btus/ft^3).
5. If one happens every hour that's **136,140 btus/day**.

This is over 30 gallons of heating oil a months just from infiltration. Compare this to 91,440 btus/day from energy passing through the walls and ceiling and you begin to realize infiltration of air is a major energy concern. In this case it accounts for 60% of heat lost.

Are there ways to reduce this? Right now for a house that's pretty efficient we are losing over 227,000 btus every day. In a month that's equivalent to 49 gallons of heating oil. Although I've seen worse, when we think of setting up a house to be as self-sufficient as possible, the less energy we can spend, the less we will have to "earn." Can we do better? – Yes!

Recovery & Heat Exchangers

Not only can you reduce the amount of energy leaving the house through the walls and ceilings, you can *recover* energy from air and water that is leaving. Most energy that is lost is lost in heat. If we can keep as much heat in the house as possible, we will significantly reduce the energy leaving.

Air

Let's go back to those air exchanges. We said one air exchange an hour is healthy. We don't want to compromise health so we will plan on one an hour. It's a shame to lose all the heat in the air just because we need to change it. What if we could keep the heat inside but still change air? It could save a lot of energy in a day. We can!

If the house has been carefully sealed so virtually no air escapes, we can bring all the exchange of air through one central location. If we do this, we can *extract* heat from the warm air leaving the house and use it to heat the cool air coming in. This is the job of a heat exchanger.

The principle of a heat exchanger, whether it's for air or water, is simple. A warm fluid passes by a cool fluid (Fluid could be air or water). This warms the cooler one and cools the warmer one. It's sort of like holding a cold drink in a glass cup. Your hand begins to feel cold because the warmth from your hand is passing to the drink. Btus pass from one to another. In a heat exchanger the fluids are kept separate by a film or other material that separates them, but conducts heat well. Like the glass between your hand and the drink, heat passes through the barrier between the two flows but keeps them separate.

How much heat can you recover by passing the cold and warm streams past each other in a heat exchanger? It would seem like you could get half or 50%. If the air inside is 70°F and out it's 50°F it would seem the out going air would raise 10°F and the incoming air would cool 10°F. We would lose 10°F per cubic foot of air but keep the other half. This is better than losing all the heat. In reality heat exchangers can do even better than 50% efficiency.

There are air heat exchangers that are between 60% and 75% efficient and hot water heat exchangers that can recover 60%.

To get more than 50% efficiency we take advantage of the fact that heat rises. Whether it's a tank of water or room of air heat still rises. At the top there is more heat than at the bottom. The secret to get above 50% is the way we design the two streams to pass.

Here is a hypothetical example.

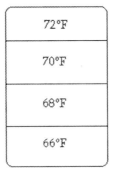

Tank of air

There are four sections in a tank. The top quarter is 72°F, the second 70°F, the third 68°F, and the last at the bottom 66°F. The cold air is 40°F.

If we run cold air through the top first here is what we get:

1. The incoming air at 40°F through the first section at 72°F results in incoming air now 56°F (half way between).
2. Incoming air 56°F through second section at 70°F results in incoming air 63°F
3. Incoming air 63°F through third section at 68°F results in incoming air 65.5°F
4. Incoming air 65.5°F through fourth section at 66°F results in incoming air 66°F

Can we exchange more energy if we run the process the other way? Let find out.

1. The incoming air at 40°F through the first section at 66°F results in incoming air now 53°F.
2. Incoming air 53°F through second section at 68°F results in incoming air 60°F
3. Incoming air 60°F through third section at 70°F results in incoming air 65°F
4. Incoming air 65°F through fourth section at 72°F results in incoming air 69°F

We find the cold air coming in is heated to 66°F using the first method and 69°F using the second.

Any heat exchanger will be most efficient if we run the cool fluid past the coolest part of the warm fluid first. This will warm the cool fluid the most. This is the most important principle of heat exchangers.

The second consideration when designing or buying a heat exchanger is how fast the heat exchanges. If the fluids pass too quickly they will not have time to transfer energy from one to another. You can speed this up by using a material between the two fluids that conduct heat well.

Another way to make sure they have time to transfer is make the length of space they are in contact longer. The longer the time the two fluids are in contact, the more heat can transfer.

That's about it on heat exchangers. They are simple devices to save energy. But is it really worth sealing every crack and running all the air through one spot?

At 40°F we need 91,440 btu/day to keep up with the conductive losses through the walls, ceiling, floor, etc of our sample house. If we allow for one air exchange an hour and the humidity is about 70%, we will lose another 136,140 from the warm air that leaves the house (and heating the cool air that replaces it).

If we are conservative and estimate we can recover 50% of that heat through a heat exchanger, the 136,140 btus we lose through air exchange is cut in half. Only 68,070 btus are now lost. This is a savings overall of 30% off the heating bill. Now only 159,510 total btus are needed each day instead of 227,580. We cut the heating oil equivalent to 34 gallons instead of 49.

This is about all we can to do conserve energy in the area of heating. Unless a way to super-insulate the walls is invented, or a way to get more heat out of the air that is being exchanged. The only other option is to build a smaller house.

Hot Water

Now we shift gears. We have done all we can to conserve energy heating our house. Now we turn to another big energy need – hot water.

Hot water is the second largest energy need in a home. It's used to take showers, do laundry, wash dishes, etc. The simplest to conserve energy here is to use less. But there is only so much you can trim. Heat exchangers help here to.

There are essentially two ways to capture the heat from your hot water that is trying to wiggle its way out of your house – a local heat exchanger or central exchanger.

Local Heat Exchanger

A majority of the heat lost down the drain is from the shower. The average American spends 12 minutes in the shower each day. An average showerhead can pump out 3 gallons a minute. If 2 ½ of those are hot water, 30 gallons of hot water per shower is lost down the drain. That's about 18,000 btus per shower.

One way to capture some of this heat is to heat the cold water that is coming to the showerhead with the hot water going down the drain. This allows you to turn the hot water down and save energy, or get hotter water for the same price since the cold water is warmer coming in.

This is accomplished by running the cold water line around the drain of the shower. As the water runs down the pipe it loses its heat to the cold water line. Over 50% of the heat going down the drain can be recaptured and reused instantly. There are heat exchangers of this type on the market that boast up to 85% of the heat can be transferred. The advantage to this system is its simplicity. There is no need for a storage tank or any other device. The cold water is instantly heated and used. Since it is easy to install and virtually maintenance free, this is a great way to save energy.

Central Heat Exchanger

The second option should capture more of the heat escaping down the drain, but it is also more complicated. If you want to catch as much heat as possible you will need a holding tank. All wastewater with heat should be run into this tank. This includes washer, dishwasher, and shower. (The kitchen sink could be run into this tank too, although not a big source of hot water.)

In the holding tank all the heat that is trying to escape from the house is captured. A copper tube coils are run through the tank. Water coming in to the hot water heater is first run through these coils. This preheats the incoming water with the hot waste water, which reduces the energy needed to bring it up to the needed temperature. The same way the air heat exchanger works. This way 50% or more of the heat leaving the house down the drain can be recycled. Every btu captured and reused mean one less to capture from the outside. A btu saved is a btu earned.

Chapter 3

Energy Budget

Now we come to the nitty-gritty. We need an energy budget. Before we look at how much energy is out there and how to capture it, we need to know how much we need. A lot of the calculations for our sample house have been done in the previous chapter. In this chapter we will walk you through doing this for your house.

Heat

How much energy is needed to heat our house depends on the difference of temperature between inside and outside. Of course this will vary year-to-year and even day-to-day. To accurately predict how much energy you will need for heat each month, you will need a record of the average temperatures of each month in your area. These can be obtained on the Internet or from weather stations. You may even have your own records. All our heating calculations will be built on these numbers.

Here are the steps you will need to take to determine the heat part of your energy budget. We will review each one in detail:

1. Calculate per degree difference for conduction through the house (walls, windows, ceiling, and floor).
2. Calculate per degree difference for infiltration (air exchange).
3. Find the average difference in temperature for each month of the year.
4. Multiply per degree difference for each month by average difference in temperature for each month.
5. Add the results for total annual heat budget.

Conduction

The process of finding conduction (or heat transfer through material) is fairly simple. Find the r-value of every surface between the inside and outside and add them up.

It's your turn. Fill in the information for each wall of your house on the following pages. All r-values in the following table are per square foot. You can calculate each component of the wall or use the average wall r-values.

R-Values for various building materials & Components:

Material	Thickness	R-Value
2x4 stud	3 ½"	4
2x6 stud	5 ½"	6.5
2x10 joist	9 ½"	10.8
2x12 joist	11 ½"	13
Plywood	½"	0.62
Plywood	¾"	0.93
Fiberglass Bat.	3 ½"	11
Fiberglass Bat.	6"	19
Drywall	½"	0.45
Drywall	5/8"	0.56
Polyurethane	1"	6.25
2x4 wall 16" centers[1]		10.43
2x4 wall 24" centers		10.92
2x6 wall 16" centers		17.10
2x6 wall 24" centers		18.24
Windows		2 - 4

Worksheet

Outside Wall #1

Height x Width = Total wall area   _____

Windows area
(Find square feet of each window by multiplying
height x width, then add all windows and enter here)   _____

Doors
(Multiply height by width to get door square feet)   _____

True wall area
(Subtract doors and windows)   _____

To find btus lost through conduction for the total wall area we
will multiply the u-value of each component by the area. The
u-value is 1 divided by r-value.

Doors (1/ r-value) x area of doors   _____

Windows (1/r-value) x area of windows   _____

True wall (1/r-value) x true wall area   _____

Add these to get total btus per hour per degree
Fahrenheit difference in inside and outside
temperature for this wall.   _____

<u>Worksheet</u>

Outside Wall #2

Height x Width = Total wall area   _____

Windows area
(Find square feet of each window by multiplying
height x width, then add all windows and enter here)   _____

Doors
(Multiply height by width to get door square feet)   _____

True wall area
(Subtract doors and windows)   _____

To find btus lost through conduction for the total wall area we will multiply the u-value of each component by the area. The u-value is 1 divided by r-value.

Doors (1/ r-value) x area of doors   _____

Windows (1/r-value) x area of windows   _____

True wall (1/r-value) x true wall area   _____

Add these to get total btus per hour per degree
Fahrenheit difference in inside and outside
temperature for this wall.   _____

Worksheet

Outside Wall #3

Height x Width = Total wall area   _____

Windows area
(Find square feet of each window by multiplying
height x width, then add all windows and enter here)   _____

Doors
(Multiply height by width to get door square feet)   _____

True wall area
(Subtract doors and windows)   _____

To find btus lost through conduction for the total wall area we
will multiply the u-value of each component by the area. The
u-value is 1 divided by r-value.

Doors (1/ r-value) x area of doors   _____

Windows (1/r-value) x area of windows   _____

True wall (1/r-value) x true wall area   _____

Add these to get total btus per hour per degree
Fahrenheit difference in inside and outside
temperature for this wall.   _____

Worksheet

Outside Wall #4

Height x Width = Total wall area   _____

Windows area
(Find square feet of each window by multiplying
height x width, then add all windows and enter here)   _____

Doors
(Multiply height by width to get door square feet)   _____

True wall area
(Subtract doors and windows)   _____

To find btus lost through conduction for the total wall area we will multiply the u-value of each component by the area. The u-value is 1 divided by r-value.

Doors (1/ r-value) x area of doors   _____

Windows (1/r-value) x area of windows   _____

True wall (1/r-value) x true wall area   _____

Add these to get total btus per hour per degree
Fahrenheit difference in inside and outside
temperature for this wall.   _____

Worksheet

Outside Wall #5
(Some will not have a 5th wall. This only applies if your house is shaped like an "L")

Height x Width = Total wall area   _____

Windows area
(Find square feet of each window by multiplying
height x width, then add all windows and enter here)   _____

Doors
(Multiply height by width to get door square feet)   _____

True wall area
(Subtract doors and windows)   _____

To find btus lost through conduction for the total wall area we will multiply the u-value of each component by the area. The u-value is 1 divided by r-value.

Doors (1/ r-value) x area of doors   _____

Windows (1/r-value) x area of windows   _____

True wall (1/r-value) x true wall area   _____

Add these to get total btus per hour per degree
Fahrenheit difference in inside and outside
Temperature for this wall.   _____

Worksheet

Ceiling

Length x Width of house= Total ceiling area _____

Skylights area
(Find square feet of each skylight by multiplying
length x width, then add all skylights and enter here)   _____

True ceiling area
(Subtract skylights   )   _____

To find btus lost through conduction for the total ceiling area
multiply the u-value of each component by the area. The u-
value is 1 divided by r-value.

Skylights (1/r-value) x area of skylights   _____

True ceiling (1/r-value) x true ceiling area   _____

Add these to get total btus per hour per degree
Fahrenheit difference in inside and outside
Temperature for the ceiling.   _____

<u>Worksheet</u>

Floor

Length x Width = Total floor area   _____

To find btus lost through conduction for the total wall area we
will multiply the u-value of each component by the area. The
u-value is 1 divided by r-value.

Floor (1/r-value) x floor area =   _____

Add these to get total btus per hour per degree
Fahrenheit difference in inside and outside
Temperature for the floor.   _____

Now add the numbers for each component from the previous worksheets to get a total conduction number for the whole house.

Wall #1 _____

Wall #2 _____

Wall #3 _____

Wall #4 _____

Wall #5 (if needed) _____

Ceiling _____

Floor _____

Total Conduction
(in btus per degree difference in temperature) _____

This is the basic conduction number for your house. Now for any day of the year you can subtract the outside temperature from the inside temperature to get the difference, then multiply by the conduction number to find how many btus per hour you are losing from your house through conduction.

As we build a budget we don't know the temperature it will be tomorrow. However, we can find average temperatures for each month in our area and use these to predict what our needs will be. You can find the average temperature each month for your area from Weather.com and other internet resources.

Once you find your monthly averages use the worksheet on the next page to determine your annual conduction losses. Here is the worksheet for our Sample house. The temperatures are from Weather.com and the conduction # is from our calculations in the previous chapter.

Sample house in Pittsburgh

Month	Inside °F	Outside °F	Difference	Conduction #	Total btus /day	Btus /month (millions)
Jan	70	28	42	127 btus/ hr°F	128,016	3.84
Feb	70	30	40	127 btus/ hr°F	121,920	3.66
March	70	39	31	127 btus/ hr°F	94,488	2.83
April	70	49	21	127 btus/ hr°F	64,008	1.92
May	70	60	10	127 btus/ hr°F	30,480	0.91
June	70	68	2	127 btus/ hr°F	6,096	0.18
July	70	74	0	127 btus/ hr°F	0	0
Aug	70	71	0	127 btus/ hr°F	0	0
Sept	70	64	6	127 btus/ hr°F	18,288	0.55
Oct	70	53	17	127 btus/ hr°F	51,816	1.55
Nov	70	43	27	127 btus/ hr°F	82,296	2.47
Dec	70	34	36	127 btus/ hr°F	109,728	3.29
Annual	Inside-outside= difference Conduction x difference x 24 (hours) = btus/day Btus/day x 30 = btus/month					**21.20**

A observation needs to be made here. You will notice the heating needs of a house will vary a lot due to the season. When we use alternative energy sources we need to keep this in mind. Storing energy for the times you need it most is important to figure into a system.

Conduction Worksheet

Month	Inside °F	Outside °F	Difference	Conduction #	Total btus /day	Btus /month (millions)
Jan						
Feb						
March						
April						
May						
June						
July						
Aug						
Sept						
Oct						
Nov						
Dec						
Annual	Inside-outside= difference Conduction x difference x 24 (hours) = btus/day Btus/day x 30 = btus/month					

Finished! Now you have the annual btus you will loose through conduction. Enter this into the worksheet at the end of the chapter. As you may remember there is only one other element in heating losses – infiltration.

Infiltration

Infiltration takes less time to calculate than conduction. We will assume it takes 0.019 btus to heat one cubic foot of air one degree. In reality, as the table shows in the previous chapter, this changes with temperature, pressure, and humidity. However, for the degree of accuracy we need 0.019 should be adequate.

Here's the formula:

$$\text{Btus/ft}^3 \text{ x temp difference x house cubic feet x air exchanges/day}$$
$$= \text{btus lost by infiltration each day}$$

Sample House

Let's work this formula through for our sample house. As you may remember our sample house is 24 feet x 24 feet and is 17 feet high including both floors. Multiplying these together gives us 9,792 cubic feet inside.

Now that we know the cubic feet we can multiply this by how many btus we lose per cubic foot for every degree Fahrenheit difference in temperature. This is 0.019 btus/°F difference. 9,792 x 0.019 gives us 186 btus for each °F difference. We can calculate the infiltration loss for each month as follows. This is the same thing we did for conduction loss but we have an infiltration number rather than a conduction number.

Sample house in Pittsburgh
(Assumes one exchange per hour)

Month	Inside °F	Outside °F	Difference	Infiltration #	Total btus /day	Btus /month (millions)
Jan	70	28	42	186 btus/ exchange °F	187,488	5.62
Feb	70	30	40	186 btus/ exchange °F	178,560	5.36
March	70	39	31	186 btus/ exchange °F	138,384	4.15
April	70	49	21	186 btus/ exchange °F	93,744	2.81
May	70	60	10	186 btus/ exchange °F	44,640	1.34
June	70	68	2	186 btus/ exchange °F	8,928	0.27
July	70	74	0	186 btus/ exchange °F	0	0
Aug	70	71	0	186 btus/ exchange °F	0	0
Sept	70	64	6	186 btus/ exchange °F	26,784	0.80
Oct	70	53	17	186 btus/ exchange °F	75,888	2.28
Nov	70	43	27	186 btus/ exchange °F	120,528	3.62
Dec	70	34	36	186 btus/ exchange °F	160,704	4.82
Annual	Inside-outside= difference Infiltration x difference x 24 (hours) = btus/day Btus/day x 30 = btus/month					**31.07**

You will notice we lose more heat through infiltration than conduction. Conduction was only 22.2 million btus each year where infiltration is 31 million. But as you remember, there is a way to reduce this total 53.2 million btus down to less than 38 million a year. Install a heat exchanger.

If we put a heat exchanger in and run all our air exchanges through it we can keep over 50% of our heat. This will reduce the 31 million a year we lose in infiltration to 15.5 million. Sometimes you can save even more. This is a 28% savings on the total heat bill! Something to think about . . .

Now work through the infiltration worksheet for your house. Remember multiply height times width times length to get the total cubic feet of your house. Then multiply this number by 0.019 to get your infiltration number. The temperatures can be copied from the conduction worksheet.

Infiltration Worksheet

Month	Inside °F	Outside °F	Difference	Infiltration #	Total btus /day	Btus /month (millions)
Jan						
Feb						
March						
April						
May						
June						
July						
Aug						
Sept						
Oct						
Nov						
Dec						
Annual	Inside-outside= difference Infiltration x difference x 24 (hours) = btus/day Btus/day x 30 = btus/month					

Hot Water

Energy needs for hot water are mainly in three areas – shower, washing machine, and dishes.

Showers

As we mentioned earlier, here's how you calculate the btus used for each shower. Grab your 4-cup measuring cup and thermometer. Go to your bathroom and adjust the shower to the temperature and pressure you like. Now catch the shower stream with the measuring cup and take its temperature and record. Then empty the cup and fill it up again timing how long it takes to fill. Write this down too. Then turn the shower all the way cold and measure the temperature of the cold water coming in.

First we will find the difference between the two temperatures. Subtracting the cold-water temperature from the shower temperature will give us the difference. My shower temperature is 110°F and my cold water is 50°F. The difference is 60°F (110-50=60).

For every pound of water I use in my shower it will take 60 btus to heat it to the temperature I like. There are 8.333 pounds of water in a gallon. So for each gallon of water I use it will take (8.333 x 60) 500 btus.

The next step is to find out how many gallons of water are used during a shower. We will use the seconds it took to fill your cup to figure this out.

For example, it took 6 ¼ seconds to fill my 4-cup container. We multiply this by 4 to convert to gallons. (16 cups to a gallon). This gives us 25 seconds to fill a gallon. Since there are 60 seconds in a minute, 60 divided by 25 gives us the flow rate in gallons per minute (g.p.m.). In my case it's 2.4 g.p.m.

Then we multiply flow rate by the 500 btus/gallon we found earlier we get btus per minute. In this case it's 1,200 btus.

Shower temp – cold water temp	= Difference temp
Difference temp x 8.333	= btus per gallon
60 / (Seconds to fill 4-cups x 4)	= Gallons per minute
btus per gallon x gallons per minute	= btus per minute
btus per minute x shower length	= btus per shower

From here it's easy to find the btus used for each shower. Just multiply the btus per minute by how many minutes it takes to take a shower.

If you don't want to do all these calculation you can use a standard 1,200 btus per minute. The average shower is 12 minutes, which gives us a standard btu use per shower of 14,400 btus if the water flow is 2.4 g.p.m.

Monthly Showers and Btu Use

People	Showers	btus
1	30	432,000
2	60	864,000
3	90	1.29 mil
4	120	1.73 mil
5	150	2.16 mil
6	180	2.59 mil

(Standard 12-minute shower)

Enter how many btus you will need for showers each month into the worksheet at the end of this section. Use the chart at the left or customize the btu use for your situation. One simple way to save energy is take a shorter shower or buy a showerhead that restricts the water flow.

Washing Machine

Like the shower you can measure how much hot water your particular washing machine is using. However it may be easier to use a general number. Each load using a hot/cold setting uses about 30 gallons of hot water. Some of the newer machines do better than this but as a general rule 30 gallons is a good guess.

Using the 500 btus per gallon calculation from the shower example means we will use about 15,000 btus for each wash. You can save money by using a warm/cold setting or by reducing the size setting on the washer when you run a smaller load. You could even do away with the washer all together, but I've found that of all the modern conveniences, a washing machine is worth it. It's a lot of work washing clothes by hand. If you're going to save, get rid of its partner the dryer. It's easy to setup a clothesline outside or in the basement with a fan.

Enter how many washes you do a month into the worksheet at the end of this section. Like the shower you can customize this if you want more exact numbers. However, 15,000 btus per wash is a good average guesstimate.

Dishwasher

Another major hot water consumer is the dishwasher. You can do without if you choose. Washing by hand uses around 7-8 gallons of hot water where a dishwasher uses 15-20.

Miscellaneous

Lastly, you will need some hot water for hand washing etc. To be safe you may want to plan about 10 gallons a day for washing hands, and any other minor needs. Here's my worksheet

Use	Times/mo	Btu use	Total
Shower	90	14,400	1,296,000
Washer	30	15,000	450,000
Dishes	90	4,000	360,000
Misc	30	5,000	150,000
Total btus			**2,256,000**

If we put in a gray water heat exchanger and are able to recover even 50% of the energy going down the drain, our hot water energy needs are suddenly reduced to **1,128,000 btus** per month!

Here is your blank worksheet. Work out your hot water needs for your house then divide in two if you choose to install a gray water heat exchanger.

Use	Times/mo	Btu use	Total
Shower			
Washer			
Dishes			
Misc.			
Total btus			

Gray water exchanger btu use: _____

Electricity

The last energy consideration is electricity. We will not be using the units of btus, although we could. (We learned from chapter 1 there are 3,414.4 btus for each Kilowatt-hour.) A more common unit is the Kilowatt-hour or kWh. It is the energy of 1,000 watts over an hour of time. This is what you see on your electric bill. Mine says I get to pay $0.11 for each one I use.

When we think about electricity there are major energy hogs and minor ones. Each one can be identified by how many watts it uses. If you have an electric hot water heater it will draw about 4,500 watts or 4.5 kilowatts (kW). If it's on for an hour it uses 4.5 kWh (kilowatt-hours). If you pay the same $0.11 I do it will cost you about $0.50. Incidentally, it costs about $0.55 to heat 30 gallons for a shower or laundry. As we will learn there are less expensive ways to get hot water than electricity.

Another major energy consumer is the clothes dryer. It pulls about 4,000 watts for its 40 to 60 minutes of drying time. This means an energy use of 2.7 to 4 kWh.

The most efficient option is to find somewhere in your house or outside where you can hang a clothesline. It's not quite as convenient as a dryer but much more energy efficient. If your line is inside a small fan uses a faction of the electricity as a dryer and does a pretty good job. If you do hang your clothes somewhere inside it needs to be a well ventilated place. The moisture coming out of the clothes needs to go somewhere.

For those who are producing their own electricity another concern in the refrigerator. It doesn't draw a huge load, less than 500 watts, but it is constant. If you don't have a dishwasher, electric clothes dryer, or electric hot water heater, the refrigerator will be your main electricity consumer. Second is the washer, but only about 0.5 kWh per load. At my prices that's 6 cents. Not a huge concern.

Here is a list of various appliances and their electricity use. As you can see if you get rid of the big ones your electricity use will fall fast.

Appliance	Watts load	kWh Used
Dryer	4,000	2.7 to 4
Refrigerator	500	5 per day
Washer	1,000 part time	0.5 per wash
Electric Heater	1,500	1.5 per hour
Toaster	1,000	0.08 per use
Oven	2,000	2.0 per hour
Stove top burner	1,000	1.0 per hour
Hair Dryer		0.08 per use
Clothes Iron		0.24 per use
TV	280	0.28 per hour
Incandescent Light	100	1.2 per 12 hours
Florescent Light	23	0.28 per 12 hours

(These are only estimates. Each model varies.)

Let's take a sample electrical budget. We will get our hot water from somewhere other than electricity. We will dry our clothes on the line, and wash dishes by hand. The refrigerator will be run off solar or wood energy (which we will explain later.) We have eliminated the big ones. What do we have left?

The washing machine will take ½ a kWh per load. 7 loads a week is 3 ½ kWh gives us 15.2 kWh each month.

The only other concern is lights. The standard incandescent light bulb is better at producing heat than light. In fact when you consider a 23 watt florescent will put out the same light as a 100 watt incandescent you realize three-fourth of the energy of an incandescent bulb is going to heat. If you switch all your lights to florescent the energy needs for lighting is cut 75%!

Lighting needs really depend on your lifestyle. If you or your family are home during the day you will use a lot more light than if you gone.

For our sample house I will budget three lights on for 16 hours a day and one light on for 8 hours at night. This is just a guess but seems like a reasonable one. Again, your needs may be significantly different.

Adding all the hours up for my lights gives me 56 light bulb hours. I will use the more efficient 23 watt fluorescents which is an energy use of 1.29 kWh per day. (56 hours x 23 watts per bulb).

I will also add one kilowatt-hour per day for miscellaneous such as hair dryer, microwave. Although these appliances can draw between 1,000 to 2,000 watts of power, we generally use them for such a short time they don't add a lot to the overall budget.

Sample Electrical Budget Worksheet

Use	Per Day (kWh)	Per Month (kWh)
Washer	0.5	15.0
Lights	1.29	38.7
TV	0.84	25.2
Miscellaneous	1.0	30
Total	**3.63**	**108.9**

Now it's your turn. Here is a worksheet for your lifestyle.

Electrical Budget Worksheet

Use	Per Day (kWh)	Per Month (kWh)

Summary

So we've made our budget for the sample house.

Month	Total Heat (conduction & infiltration)	Hot Water	Electricity
Jan	9.47 million	1,128,000	109
Feb	9.01 million	1,128,000	109
Mar	6.99 million	1,128,000	109
Apr	4.73 million	1,128,000	109
May	2.25 million	1,128,000	109
Jun	0.45 million	1,128,000	109
Jul	0	1,128,000	109
Aug	0	1,128,000	109
Sep	1.35 million	1,128,000	109
Oct	3.83 million	1,128,000	109
Nov	6.08 million	1,128,000	109
Dec	8.11 million	1,128,000	109
Total	52.28 million	13.54 million	1,308 kWh

Not bad. In real life this may be more or less. The above is doable. It just takes some careful planning. If we get our heat and hot water from oil, and electricity from the grid our energy bill would be less than $160 a month (at 2006 prices).

But why get the energy from retailers when there is energy all around us? Now that we know how much we need let's find out where it is, how much is there, and how to get it.

Energy Budget

Transfer the total from each of the worksheets in this chapter to the space below. You will have to add the conduction and infiltration together to get total btus needed each month for heat. This will give you one place for future reference. All units are btus except electricity, which is in kWh.

I need:

Month	Total Heat (conduction & infiltration)	Hot Water	Electricity
Jan			
Feb			
Mar			
Apr			
May			
Jun			
Jul			
Aug			
Sep			
Oct			
Nov			
Dec			
Total			

Part II – Where's the Energy?

Chapter 4

Hydro

Hydro power works a lot like your pulley system that let you down 100 feet from the tree. We are taking advantage of the fact that water falls. We could take rocks or trees from the top of mountains, harness them to a cable and as they slide down the hill let that cable turn a generator. However, eventually we would run out of rocks and trees at the top of all the mountains.

Water has it's own system of getting to the top of the mountain through rain and we don't have to expend the energy to get it there. However, we can take advantage of its energy as it falls.

There are two ways to get energy from moving water. The high head method is used for water that has a significant drop in elevation. It's called "high head" because of the high "head" pressure it exerts from its descent. The other method is low head or *run of river*. It involves extracting energy from a river or stream passing by.

High Head

To calculate the power available in water that drops in elevation we go back to the idea of foot-pounds. Every pound of water that falls one foot contributes one foot-pound of energy to the system. If we can get 33,000 foot-pounds of water to fall in one minute we have one horsepower of energy.

For instance, there is a four-acre piece of property for sale, which I've had my eye on. A creek runs down the hill with a vertical drop of about 150 feet. I went out there just to see what kind of power I could get from the creek.

By filling a bucket and using my stopwatch I estimate the water flows at 80 gallons a minute. Here is how you calculate the power in this stream.

1. First find how many pounds of water fall in one minute. You may remember there are 8.333 lbs of water in each gallon. We have 80 gallons in one minute. 80 gallons x 8.333 lbs/gallon = 667 pounds per minute of water flow.

2. To find foot-pounds we multiply how many pounds fall by the distance in feet. 667 lbs of water/minute x 150 feet of drop = 100,050 foot-lbs/minute.

3. Electricity is usually measured in kilowatts or kilowatt-hours. There are 44,254 foot-lbs/minute per kilowatt. 100,050 foot-lbs per minute / 44,254 = 2.26 kilowatts.

4. To find kilowatt-hours (kWh) for each day we multiply by the hours in a day (assuming the creek runs 24 hours a day). 2.26 kW x 24 = 54.24 kWh each day. (Notice Kilowatts (kW) becomes kilowatt-hours (kWh) by measuring the power output over time).

As we will see this is plenty of power to run a house that uses its energy wisely. We estimated a need of about 109 kWh of electricity for a whole month. At this rate we could get all our electricity needs in two days! However, all of the energy in the creek can't be captured because whatever collector we use is not 100% efficient. The good news is, even if you can capture 50% you would still have 813 KWh/month – over seven times our needs.

You can do these calculations for any water flow over any vertical drop by remembering there are 8.333 lbs of water per gallon. The same principle of foot-pounds applies whether it's water or rocks or you coming down from a tree.

Low Head

Just because you don't have water that drops doesn't mean you can't use hydropower. Water passing can be mined for energy too. However, since the energy doesn't come from a drop in elevation we have to calculate the power available in a different way.

Gathering energy from water passing or from the *run of the river*, as it is sometimes called, works a lot like gathering energy from wind. The trick is to figure out how much pressure is being exerted on the collector and how much surface area it has.

Instead of calculating the pressure the water exerts we will use a constant. It's easier to make calculations from the speed of the water if the weight and pressure is already calculated for you. Here is the formula for calculating how much electricity you can get from a collector. Remember, collectors are not 100% efficient. In fact, plan on getting about 50% of what you calculate.

The energy available cubes as the speed of the water doubles. We talk more about this when we look at wind power. Here's the formula.

Power in watts = 4.3184 x (velocity in feet per second)^3 x (surface area of collector in square feet)

For a collector with a circle shaped surface facing upstream you can find the area by multiplying the radius (from center to outside of the circle) by itself, then multiply by 3.1415. This is the formula to find the area of a circle.

Here's an example. I make a collector. It's a sealed generator with a blade. My plan is to place it under water and as the river passes it will turn the blade, then turn the generator. The river runs only 3 feet per second (about 2 miles per hour) and my blade is 1 ½ feet radius. How much power can I get?

63

- ❖ $4.3184 \times (3 \text{ feet/second})^3 = 116.6$ watts per ft^2
- ❖ $3.1415 \times 1.5^2 = 7.068 \text{ ft}^2$
- ❖ $7.07 \times 116.6 = 824$ watts. 412 usable watts.

That's enough power to keep a refrigerator and lights going. If you had to you could survive on that.

Uses

Usually home hydropower is not used for heating because there is not enough of it. Electricity is the main use. However, it could be if someone had an over abundance of hydropower. In the above example we could use the extra-generated power to supply some of our heating needs. We are only using 109 kWh per month of electricity. That leaves 704 kWh for heat. At 3414 btus per kilowatt, we could generate 2.4 million btus for heat. As you may recall our heating needs for the sample house average 4.4 million btus a month. This would give over half the heat needed for the month.

If we use the extra electricity from our hydro plant for hot water, it would well cover the 1.13 million btus needed. Of course most hydroelectric systems can't produce this much, or have a higher need for electricity. If you find yourself in this situation consider yourself lucky.

Chapter 5

Solar

The sun gives off an incredible amount of energy. Without it life would not exists on earth. At the top of our atmosphere each square foot is receiving about 433 btus of power per hour. That's about 127 watts per square foot per hour. If I could absorb all that energy with the south side of my house (which is 552 ft^2) I could have 70 kWh of energy in one hour. In a 12 hour day I could absorb enough energy to supply the electrical needs of the sample house (3.7 kWh/day) for 227 days!

Before we get too excited about this there are two factors that will make the energy actually getting to the side of my house much lower. They are atmosphere and angle.

Atmosphere is the stuff we live in and breath. Piled on top of us, staying there from the pull of gravity, is air. In fact for every square inch of surface area there are 14.7 pounds of air pushing against it. (I have a theory this is why I'm so tired, but few are willing to listen). Through that atmosphere come the rays of the sun to give us, and the whole earth, energy. As it does it hits dust particle and moisture in the air. Some is reflected back into space. The rest makes its journey to the earth's surface where it is absorbed as heat or reflected back into space.

How much gets here to be used? Atmospheric conditions vary some across the United States; so to say exactly how much will reach me will depend on actually measuring it at my house. But we can get a good idea within a tolerance of 10%.

How many btus strikes a surface perpendicular to the sun each hour depends on the angle of the sun to the earth. When the sun is at a lower angle on the horizon (such as rising or setting) it's light has to travel through much more of the atmosphere. In fact when it is setting or rising so much of its energy is diffused in the atmosphere we can actually look at the sun with the naked eye. Without this low angle we could never do this.

If the sun is directly overhead we can calculate how many btus per hour we would receive on a clear day. (The sun never is directly overhead in the United States except for part of Florida and Texas for a short time in June at noon.) Taking into account a rough guess at atmospheric conditions we can get a close idea how much energy would get to us.

We know the constant outside the atmosphere is **433 btus** per hour per ft^2. The length of the atmosphere on a clear day when the sun is straight up absorbs or reflects about 68 btus. Substracting 68 from 433 gives us a constant to work with. **365 btus** per hour per ft^2 reaches us. As we said before, this is an estimate as atmospheric conditions change. For more accurate data refer to NASA's measurements for your latitude and longitude. Currently this can be found at http://eosweb.larc.nasa.gov/cgi-bin/sse/sse.cgi?na+s01#s01. If this is out of date an updated link should be on our website at www.AlternativeEnergyBasics.com

We now have all the figures to calculate the btus received for any angle. We've calculated that one atmosphere straight up will still give us 365 $btus/ft^2/hour$. This is 84.3% of the original energy at the top of the atmosphere.

To calculate the sun's btu output at any elevation (degrees rise from the horizon) the formula is:

$$\textbf{BTU output per hour per } ft^2 = S * L^A$$

Where:
        S is the Solar Constant of 433 btu/hr ft^2
        L is 0.843, the amount of energy left after passing
        through the atmosphere at 90°.
        A is the $Sine^{-1}$ of the angle of elevation.

For example, it is a clear day and the sun is about 30° from the horizon. How many btus can I get for each square foot that is perpendicular to the sun's rays? "S" and "L" are constants. The inverse sine of 30° is 2. So we get 307 btus/hr ft^2.

You can make an angle measuring tool by attaching a weight to a piece of string and taping the other end at the zero angle of a carpenter's quick square. Sight down the square at the sun, then read the angle off the side.

This formula can be used for any angle. As the earth turns the angle between the sun and horizon will change throughout the day. Day to day it will changes with the seasons. The easiest way to calculate the output at the moment is to use an angle-measuring tool. Here is a table that has already been calculated.

Table of sun angles and btus per hour

Angle	BTU/hr	Angle	BTU/hr	Angle	BTU/hr
1	0	13	203	30	308
2	3	14	214	35	321
3	17	15	224	40	332
4	37	16	233	45	340
5	61	17	241	50	346
6	85	18	249	55	352
7	107	19	256	60	356
8	127	20	263	65	359
9	145	21	269	70	361
10	162	22	274	75	363
11	177	23	280	80	364
12	190	24	285	85	365
		25	289	90	365

But all this hardly helps when predicting the btus available next month, or knowing where the angle will be throughout the year. Few of us have the time to go outside and take measurements every hour, every day for the year. Clouds make this impossible anyway. How do I predict where the sun will be at a certain hour on a certain day? How do I know how much energy is given through the whole day?

Average btus per day

When we set up a solar energy collection system the most useful data to us is how many btus each day our site will receive for each square foot of surface area. Once we know this it's easy to figure out how big the collector should be, and where we want it. But finding how many btus we get each day can be tricky. We can tract the sun across the sky, then add up the btus for each hour of the day and each day of the year. But since the sun changes every day, we would have to do this for each day of the year. As we said, cloudy days present a problem since we don't get all the energy we can on sunny days.

Unless you are merely interested in the track of the sun and like to do long and complicated calculations there is a better way. There is a National Solar Radiation Data Base you can access through the web to get solar data for your area. Most of the data is in watts per square meter per day. To convert to btus per square foot multiply watts per square meter by 317.1.

The National Solar Radiation Data Base can be found here:
http://rredc.nrel.gov/solar/old_data/nsrdb/redbook/sum2/state.html

A map of the same data can be found here:
http://www.windsun.com/Solar_Basics/Solar_maps.htm

You will find several types of data for your location.

Websites change periodically. If these are not active you can get the latest link at our website. AlternativeEnergyBasics.com

Collectors

It is easy to produce heat with the sun. Paint something flat black and leave it out in the sun and you will have made a collector. Some of the simplest heat collectors are made in just this way. A black hose snaked across the ground in the sun can be a preheater for the main water heater. For every degree Fahrenheit a gallon of water is raised, that's 8 1/3 less btus used by the water heater to bring it up to temperature. A water tank could be painted flat black and have the same result.

One of the challenges of producing heat from the sun is keeping it. The hose snaked across the ground is losing some of its heat to the air that passes by. If there was a material that allowed the sun's rays to shine through, but stopped the air from convecting the heat away, it would be helpful in our pursuit for a good collector.

Of course there are materials like this. Glass, plexiglass, and others. If we put our black hose now under glass we can capture the sun's rays, but stop the air from transporting our heat away.

But there is another enemy – Conduction. The hose is still laying on the ground. The ground is absorbing some of our heat too. What if we laid it instead on a sheet of polystyrene to insulate it from the ground? That way we wouldn't lose so much heat. And so we do, and sincel we are at it we build a box on the sides of our hose and put glass over it to keep the heat in.

So we have a black hose under glass in an insulated box. But the hose really doesn't have that much surface area in the sun. It snakes back and forth through our box. What if we had enough hose to cover the bottom of the box? That way all the light from the sun coming in would be absorbed. So we do, but instead of using a hose we use copper pipe. Instead of covering the whole bottom of our box with copper pipe we use an aluminum sheet and attach our copper pipe to it. This way all the heat from the sun hits the aluminum. Since aluminum conducts heat well it transfers this heat to the copper pipe, which transfers it to the water inside our house.

So we have an insulated box with glass and a surface covering the space inside so all the rays of the sun can be collected. Our garden hose has improved. But there is still two ways we can improve our simple collector.

For little extra cost we could install reflectors around the collector to reflect some of the surrounding light in. We wouldn't have to build a bigger collector but with reflectors put more light on the collector. Catch more light and in essence increase the surface we are collecting from.

The other improvement we could make is get rid of the air around the aluminum collector inside our box. Even air that is still will conduct heat. What if the heat couldn't even escape through the air? So we suck all of the air out and seal it. Now we have the best collector we can get.

This is the basics of a solar heat collector. They are all variation on the basic idea. Evacuated tubes achieve a higher heat capture rate than the flat panel collector we started with. There are others which use some kind of reflector to concentrate the solar energy on a specific point. Much higher temperatures can be achieved this way. But with higher temperatures comes a higher difference between the temperature inside the collector and outside, which means more heat loss through the insulation.

The other consideration when designing or buying a solar collector is orientation. A flat panel facing directly at the sun will collect the most energy. However, the sun moves which presents a dilemma. You can install a tracking system, which points the collector at the sun at all times. Or you can adjust the collector so that it points most directly at the sun in the hottest part of the day.

The data from the National Solar Radiation Data Base gives you data for a flat panel laying flat, at 90°, and 15° on either side of the angle of your latitude. They also have data for concentrating

Solar Noon

At times it's helpful to know where the sun will be at a certain time of day and also know where and when it will be highest. This is especially helpful when installing solar collectors.

To figure this out we first have to understand a concept called *Solar Noon.*

Every 4 minutes the earth turns one degree. There are 360° total around the earth. These are marked in longitudinal lines. Every hour the earth turns 15°.

To find solar noon in your area you will need to know your longitude. This is easily found on a map of your area, or by finding your location on earth's surface with a GPS unit. If you have already downloaded the National Solar Radiation Data for your location you will have this information at the top of your data sheet.

For each time zone, there is a place where solar noon is the actual time. For the rest of us, we have to correct for it.[i] If you are in the Eastern Time zone this is at 75° longitude. If you are east of this you will have to add 4 minutes for every degree difference. If you are west you will have to subtract 4 minutes for every degree. In the Central Time Zone solar noon is correct at 90° longitude. Mountain Time at 105°, and Pacific Time at 120°. These are all Standard Time. If you are using Daylight Savings Time you will have to correct to Standard Time.

There is one more correction that will need to be done. The earth is not steady in its orbit. Because of this the actual time the sun is the highest changes by a few minutes through the year. Once you have calculated solar noon for your longitude, use the chart below to correct for the time of year. This will give you solar noon in your area down to the minute.

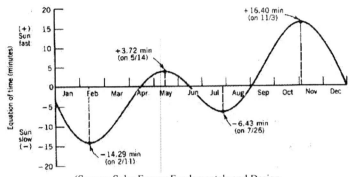

(Source: Solar Energy Fundamentals and Design
by W. Stine and R. Harrigan, John Wiley 1985. Used by permission.)

Another way to find solar noon for a particular day is to obtain an accurate sunrise/sunset table for your location. The time exactly between these two is solar noon.

At solar noon the sun will be directly true south. Once you find this location you can calculate where the sun will be at other times of the day.

For every minute the suns passes due south it will be 0.25° or ¼° off true south. For example, we have calculated the time of solar noon (the time when the sun is highest and directly true south). Now it's 65 minutes past solar noon. What direction will the sun be and how many degrees will it be off solar noon?

Hour Angle = 0.25 x 65 minutes.

The answer is 16.25° past solar noon. Since solar noon occurs when the sun at a direction of 180°, adding 16.25° gives us 196.25°.

We could calculate this for times before solar noon too. What if the time is 65 minutes before solar noon? The same formula applies, we just subtract 16.25° from 180° instead of adding it to get 163.75°.

By the way, the sun always rises and sets at the same bearing angle off due south. If the suns rises 87° left of due south (true) it will set 87° right of due south.

Making Electricity

Electricity can be made by using heat from the sun. If you can get water hot enough to turn to steam, you can drive a generator. Parabolic mirrors have been used to focus the sun's rays on a pipe. This pipe then turns the water inside it to steam, which runs a generator that produces electricity. The same concept has been used with a dish, like a satellite dish with a collector at the focal point. The heat produced is used to produce electricity.

The collector you choose will depend on use. If you want electricity from the sun you may choose to use the photovoltaic solar panel. It is the simplest way at the moment for a homeowner to take advantage of the sun for electricity. But with a return of 12-14% of the energy striking it, it may not be the most efficient way.

If there were some way to produce electricity from heat in a fairly efficient way, we would be in good shape. Heat can be found easily from the sun or wood or oil or propane, etc. Heat is not hard to produce. Electricity, on the other hand, is relatively hard to produce. If only we could easily do this . . . Maybe you can be the one who invents a way.

Chapter 6

Wind

The energy in wind can be deceptive. The wind blowing at 1 mph has 0.11 watts of energy for every square foot of surface area. That's not much. However, this amount doesn't double when you get to two mph, it cubes or increases by the third power. So that lowly 0.11 watts per square foot of surface area at 1 mph is eight times more (0.88 watts) at 2 mph. At 10 mph it's 110 watts and at 20 mph, the energy in the wind is 880 watts/ft^2.

These calculations are based on dry air at standard pressure and temperature.   In reality the density of the air changes with temperature, humidity, and elevation.

Elevation: Density and therefore energy available **decreases** as altitude increases.

Temperature: Density and energy available **decreases** as temperature increases.

Humidity: Density and energy available **increases** as humidity increases.

These variables could change the calculated power available by as much as 25%. However, the following formula should give you a fairly good idea of how much energy is there. A change is a few miles per hour could change the value even more than 25%, so this accuracy should be tolerable.

Power in Watts = (Wind speed in mph)^3 x 0.11

Usually wind energy is captured by some kind of wind turbine that has a circular area. The following formula may be helpful to calculate the power available to a certain sized wind turbine.

Power in Watts = (Wind speed in mph)^3 x 0.11 x Π r^2

Where
r = radius (or half the width) of the circle in feet.
Π = 3.14159

For example, if a wind was blowing at 10 mph and the blade length of our turbine is 2 feet the math would look like this:

$$10^3 \text{ x } 0.11 \text{ x } 3.14159 \text{ x } 2^2 = 1,382 \text{ watts}$$

Of course any turbine is not 100% efficient. You can expect to get about 30% of the energy available.

Like hydropower, wind power is usually used for electricity. Electricity is the hardest energy of the three main energy needs to obtain, so any way we can get energy into the form of electricity we tend to keep it there. There is the possibility that you would find yourself with an over abundance in your situation. Electricity is easy to transfer to heat with an efficiency of about 95%.

Wind is not often constant, so time of production and time of use don't often meet. This requires some kind of storage system. Certainly a factor when considering this option.

Collectors

The most common type of collector of wind energy is the wind turbine. This is a large blade, like an airplane propeller turned in the wind. Designed right these can be highly efficient, taking so much of the winds energy, if you stand behind them you are in calm air. They are most efficient at the wind speed they are designed for. This makes knowing what kind of wind patterns to expect important for success. Recording data about wind patterns in your area takes time since wind patterns can vary in just a few miles due to terrain, so gathering data from a weather station in the area may not be accurate.

There are other types of collectors. Some have used a couple 55 gallon barrels cut lengthwise as the fins to their collector. An advantage to this is that the wind can come from any direction and still turn the collector.

You may have some ideas of your own or may want to buy an already made system. As long as you understand how much wind you have and the power behind it you can set up the right system to do the job.

Chapter 7

Wood

When we burn wood, in a sense, we are using the energy from the sun. Every plant takes sunshine (light) and carbon dioxide from the air and creates itself. The oxygen is released for us and other mammals to breath. We take that oxygen into our lungs, combine it with carbon from the *plants* we have eaten (even in meat the carbon originally came from plants) and release it in the form of carbon dioxide. When our bodies combine a carbon atom and two oxygen atoms to form carbon dioxide, the reaction gives off energy our bodies use. The carbon dioxide is then used again by the plant. The plant needs energy to separate the atoms of carbon and oxygen to build itself and again gets this energy from the sun.

So in a sense plants are storage for the suns energy. The energy is released when we eat the plants, and it is released when a plant decays or is burned.

Trees are big storage containers made up of carbon from the air. That carbon will be released by rot or by burning. Why not make use of the energy and burn it?

How much energy is in wood? According to *Thomas J. Glover's Pocket Ref*, quite a lot. The following is assuming an efficiency of 55% and is million btus per cord.

Ash	12.3	Maple	11.9
Aspen	9.1	Oak	14.5
Beech	12.8	Lodgepole	10.6
Birch	11.9	Pinion Pine	18.4
Cherry	11.7	White Pine	8.0
Cottonwood	8.7	YellowPine	12.1
Douglas Fir	14.5	Red Cedar	10.9
Elm	10.9	Spruce	8.8
Hemlock	9.3	Willow	7.2

One cord is the amount of wood that will fit in a space 4' x 4' x 8', or 128 ft^3. Wood can vary quite a bit in usable btus depending on moisture content. This assumes 20% moisture content. This means 20% of the woods weight is water.

As you can see, what kind of wood you use will determine how many times you go to the wood box. For instance, Pinion Pine has twice the btus as spruce.

Heat

Wood is most commonly used for heating. A woodstove has heated many a house. It's reliable and in many areas plentiful.

Wood may be the best option for you to heat your house. The

To test how much moisture is in wood, shave some chips of the wood and weigh them. Put them in an oven at about 200°F for an hour. Weigh them again, and then put them in for another hour. Continue do to this until they stop losing weight. This is the dry weight.

Dividing the dry weight by the wet weight will give the percentage of dry weight. Subtract this from 100 will give the percent moisture content of the wood.

For example, a wet sample is 10 oz. After it dries it weighs 8 oz. If we divide 8 by 10 we get 0.80. 80% of the weight is from the wood. The other 20% is water.

advantage is the independence it brings. Other sources of energy rely on the wind blowing, the sun shining, etc. Wood is always there.

Of course wood heat is a lot of work. There is an old adage, "Wood warms you twice, once while cutting and twice when burning." It is not *free*, but if you have more time then money it may be a good choice.

One disadvantage of a wood stove is the need to attend it and the mess it makes from hauling wood into the house and the ash that may spill. But some of these disadvantages can be removed by using a central wood boiler.

The concept is simple. Instead of using the air around a wood stove to heat the house, use the heat from the wood stove to heat a water jacket around the stove. This water then can be stored or used immediately for heat. Of course we can get our hot water this way too.

The advantages are tremendous. The boiler can be outside or in a basement. No need for wood chips all over the living room rug. It's easy to transport water through pipes to the place where you need the heat. With a wood stove many times the back bedroom is cold while the room the stove is in is too hot. A well regulated heat is convenient. A water based heat system lends well to a backup oil or gas fired boiler too. Just a few extra plumbing valves allows for a backup system to kick on anytime the temperature in the primary wood boiler drops below a certain point.

One of the challenges to wood heat is to achieve the efficient burning temperature of wood. Wood burns most efficiently at higher temperatures. If too many btus are drawn away too quickly the wood will not burn well. So the challenge comes in taking the heat, but not too much of the heat away too soon.

One way to over come this is a heat storage tank. If there is a heat storage tank in the system, a hot fire can be made for a few hours and the heat stored in the tank. Then the heat from the storage can heat the house the rest of the day. This also cuts down on the constant need to refuel a fire.

Hot Water

Hot water can be produced from wood at a reasonable cost. When competing against electric or gas water heat it is well worth it. Even if not all of the heat is gained from wood, preheating the water before it is heated in a conventional way could save a lot of money each month.

To design a wood hot water system we need to first decide how much hot water is needed. The faster the water flows from the holding tank to the stove and back to the holding tank, the more hot water you will receive. This is due to the temperature difference between the surface of the stove where the heat is being collected and the water. You may remember our previous discussion on r-value. Each material has a certain r-value. This is the number of btus that will pass through a square foot of it in an hour for each degree difference of each side. If there is a large difference more heat will pass. It works the same way for heating water from a wood stove. The greater the difference in temperature between the stove and the water, the more heat will transfer.

If your hot water tank is close enough to your stove you can actually create what is called a thermo-siphon. Hot water like hot air rises. By taking advantage of this fact you can create a natural circulation through the heat exchanger on the stove and your hot water tank. The higher you put the tank above the stove, the hotter the water inside will be. The lower the tank, the cooler it will be. If you choose to go this way, you will want to experiment to find the right temperature for your hot water tank.

Electricity

One of the least efficient transfers in the energy world is to turn heat into electricity. It can be done with what's called a thermocouple but the amount of heat energy out compared to the electrical energy received is not much.

One way to get electricity from heat is to reach a high enough temperature to boil water (212°F at sea level). Once the water turns into steam, pressure is created which can turn a small turbine or piston engine and produce electricity through a generator. The efficiency is about 30%.

Another way to get electricity from wood is through a wood gasifier. During World War II gasoline was scarce in Europe. Many turned to wood and other bio mass products as a source of fuel.

The basics are simple. When wood burns most of what you see burning is not the wood at all but the gases that are being released. These gases release in the heat of the fire. It takes about 500°F to release them. You can do this yourself by using a magnifying lens in the sun. The gases will begin to release in the heat, then suddenly they will catch on fire. (A Fresnel magnifying lens works well.) You can also take chips of wood and heat them in an old pressure cooker until they reach the right temperature and light the exiting gas. However, this is not recommended. If oxygen is present in the pressure cooker the whole thing could explode!

This in its simplest form is a wood gasifier. To make use of it, the gas is then pumped to an internal combustion engine with some modification of the carburetor. This powers the engine to produce electricity or run your car down the road.

One of the issues of a wood gasifier is the charcoal it leaves behind. This can be a benefit if we can design a machine that would use the charcoal to heat the wood to harvest the gases. This would exclude an outside source of heat (campfire under the pressure cooker) and produce less waste.

This is the secret to a well designed gasifier.

For more information on gasifiers check out these websites:

- ❖ http://www.gengas.nu/byggbes/contents.shtml
- ❖ www.ienergyinc.com/woodgas.htm
- ❖ www.AlternativeEnergyBasics.com

Chapter 8

Other

There are many sources of power in the world. We have only looked at the more common ones. Really anything that moves could be a source of power. Exercising your horse could charge your battery bank. Some have harnessed the power of waves rolling in from the ocean. Others have used the tide.

You now know how to calculate the energy potential. If it's motion it's done the same way hydro is calculated: movement in pounds over a certain distance in feet gives units of foot-pounds.

Anything that produces a lot of heat can be used to make electricity from steam. Geothermal power has been generated this way. The heat from volcanic activity is used to produce steam and turn a turbine. As technology progresses and we find more efficient ways to get electricity from heat the options will expand.

Part III – The System

Chapter 9

Storage

At this point in time there are three main ways to store the energy we capture. There are advantages to each. It depends on what you are trying to store.

Heat Tank

If we want to store heat for hot water or heating needs for a short time, the easiest way is in the form of heat. Every time we transfer energy forms we loose some, so to store heat in its *native* form makes the most sense.

When we think of a media to store heat in, we have to think about both transportability and the most storage in the least amount of space. There is one media that is good at both –water.

That's right, water will hold a lot of heat per cubic foot of material and it is easy to transport from one place to another through piping. For space and portability I believe it is the best solution. Other can be used such as rocks, cement, etc. But they are neither portable nor hold as much heat per cubic foot.

Heating one cubic foot of water 1°F will require 62.4 btus. The good news is, when it's cooled it will give back those btus. So to size a holding tank requires we know how many btus we need to store.

Going back to our sample house we find we need 4.4 million btus a month for heating and 1.2 million for hot water. It would certainly be handy to store a month's worth of energy in the heat of water. Could this be done? If we stored the water at 200°F and let it drop to 80°F we would have 120°F of *storage space*. So each cubic foot of water would store 4,992 btus of heat (80 degrees x 62.4 btus/cubic foot). For our 5.6 million btus needed a month we would need 1,122 ft^3 of storage space. That's a square tank just over 10 x 10 x 10 feet. A pretty big tank but if we want that kind of storage it could be done.

Of course one of the considerations is to insulate a tank that size. The area would be 100 ft^2 on each side for a surface area of 600ft^2. If we stored the tank in a room at 70°F the difference would be 130°F (if the water was 200°F). If we insulated the surface with r-30 insulation, for each square foot of surface area we would lose 4 1/3 btus or 2,600 btus an hour. As the temperature went down so would the btu loss. This works out to 62,400 a day. 1.8 of the 6.5 million btus would be lost in a month.

This actually may not be a bad option considering if you stored the same energy in batteries it would be very expensive and you would only get 50% of it back. Even over a month we've only lost 28% of the energy we put in the heat tank.

There may even be better ways to insulate the tank with evacuated panels etc. Overall, it's a good way to store energy. Although, we may want to consider a smaller tank.

Batteries

The most common way to store energy is in batteries. It is not a great way due to the energy loses but it may be the best for your needs. It is beyond the scope of this book to explain how to make batteries from scratch, although for the die-hard do-it-yourselfer it is possible.

Basics of a Battery

A battery is made up of two dissimilar metals that react to produce electricity. When the battery is recharged the chemical reaction that created the electricity is reversed. Because of the way most batteries are made this discharging wears away the metal plates, which finally "wear out" the battery.

This is worse when a battery is completely discharged. If you keep the batteries above 50% charge they last much longer. So you should design your system with twice as much battery storage as you need.

Batteries can get expensive which means it may be more cost effective to design a system that uses less energy than a system with more storage.

Battery capacity is measured in amp-hours. As the name implies this is the amount of energy in one amp over a period of an hour. Like other measurements it doesn't have to be an hour.

These are 1 amp-hour:

1 amp for 60 minutes
2 amps for 30 minutes
3 amps for 20 minutes
4 amps for 15 minutes
6 amps for 10 minutes
10 amps for 6 minutes

The formula is:

Amp-hours = (amps x minutes)/ 60

The first step is to figure out how many amp-hours of storage you need? From our sample house we estimated 109 kWh a month. In a 30 day month this is 3.7 kWh a day. If you are sure to get that amount of energy from your collectors every day, you only need to store enough energy for one day (so you can have electricity during the night). Doubling the amount needed to keep the batteries above 50% charge means we would need 7.4 kWh of storage capacity.

But not only do we need extra storage capacity, batteries are not 100% efficient. In other words they don't give back to us what we put in them. Some energy is lost in heat and friction.

According to a paper by *John W. Stevens and Garth P. Corey*[ii] you can expect to get back 91% of the energy you put in when charging the battery between 0% and 84% full. However, charging a battery between 79% and 84% only is 55% efficient. Charges when a battery is 90% charged or more is less than 50% efficient.

This creates an interesting situation. You don't want your batteries discharged too much or you will wear them out. But keeping them charged towards their maximum capacity will waste energy. A well sized system becomes important.

Let's go back to our 3.7 kWh per day need for electricity. We don't want the system too big but we do want some storage since many natural energy sources are not always constant (such as at night). We will build into our system one day worth of backup.

This will require a system able to deliver 7.4 kWh of electricity (doubled to help the batteries last longer).

Looking at the math to the right we will need 617 amp-hours of storage. This would require 7 100 amp-hour batteries.

The Math

If we need 3.7 kWh storage we need to double it since our batteries need to stay above 50%. This gives us 7.4 kWh.

One Kilowatt equals 1,000 watts

7.4 kWh x 1,000 w-hours/kWh = 7,400 watt-hours.

amps = watts/volts

7,400 watt-hours / 12 volt (battery voltage) = **617 amp-hours**.

Most of the time these batteries are going to stay charged above 90% capacity, which reduces our charging efficiency below 50%. You should plan on putting in 7.4 kWh per day if you want 3.7 kWh out.

Batteries are not my favorite way to store energy. There are too many losses. But they may be the best way to have electricity on demand.

Hydrogen

There are other storage methods developing. Hydrogen is one of the most promising. It is almost the perfect storage medium. When it burns it produces water as a by-product. It can be pumped through fuel cells to produce electricity as needed. It can be produced fairly effectively through electrolysis. (You can produce it yourself with two wires, a 9-volt battery, a cup of water, and a tablespoon of baking soda. The bubbles from one wire are oxygen and the other hydrogen.)

The problem is storage in any efficient way. It either has to be put in tanks at high pressure or stored combined with another compound. Both present logistical problems.

Chapter 10

Summary

We are almost done. Since you've made it this far you know a lot more about energy than most people do. You know what energy is, and how it is measured. You know how to design a house to use energy efficiently and how to make an energy budget. You know where to find some sources of energy and how to calculate what energy is there. You also know how to store energy for future use. Hopefully by this time you have a pretty good idea what your system will look like.

Like any budget if the expenses exceed the income you have to do something. There are only two choices – cut expenses or increase income.

We hope this little book as been helpful. There is more reading to be done, but now you should know what else you need to know – that's half the battle.

Alternative energy is a fun topic. It requires creativity and a determination to beat your own path. However, that path is getting easier to beat as technology and information grow.

Enjoy your journey. If you are leaving this book with more ideas and an excited sense of what could be I am glad I wrote it.

Thanks for reading.

Endnotes:

[i] The following method will get a close time. In reality solar noon changes during the course of the year due to the earth's orbit. Depending on the day of the year it could change as much as 15 minutes. For more information on this refer to Edward Mazria excellent book, *The Passive Solar Energy Book* pages 288-9.

[ii] **A Study of Lead-Acid Battery Efficiency Near Top-of-Charge and the Impact on PV System Design**
John W. Stevens and Garth P. Corey
Sandia National Laboratories, Photovoltaic System Applications Department
Sandia National Laboratories, Battery Analysis and Evaluation Department
PO Box 5800, MS 0753
Albuquerque, New Mexico 87185-0753

Printed in the United States
213742BV00001B/55/A